PRAISE IS COMELY FOR THE UPRIGHT

By:

Apostle DR. PAMELLA RICHARDSON

TABLE OF CONTENTS

PREFACE

This book is written in the simplest manner, so that it could be understood by persons at all spiritual and intellectual levels because God says that He wants all His people to worship Him. Hopefully, we will all learn about active praise and worship whether as individuals or corporately.

The objective is to encourage, admonish and teach God's people how to celebrate Him in thanksgiving, praise and worship **in Spirit and in Truth.**

One Sunday morning, sometime in 2005, Dr. Paella Richardson was invited to preach/teach at the church where she attended at that time. The topic that the Lord put on her heart was **"Praise is Comely for the Upright".** After that Sunday, praise and worship took on a new dimension in that church.

In 2009, the Lord told her to organize a worship conference, but He said do not call it a conference because it must be experienced. He reminded me of the Seven Levels of Praise that was taught by Myles Munroe in 1983 (she still has her notes.), at a church where she attended in Trinidad.

Sometime subsequent to that the Lord said to her, write a book on Praise and Worship and title it **"Praise is Comely for the Upright".**

This is it, folks!

Dedication

Thisbook isdedicated to thememory of my mom, M rs. GeraldineRichardson.

W hen wewerekidsshemadesurethat wehad a God consciousness. Eventhough shewasnot a Christian at thetime shetaught us, her fivechildren, to pray and sentusto church every Sunday.

As I got older and gavemy heart to theLord, shealso accepted Christ asher savior and dedicated her llfeto Him.

I am eternally grateful for thefoundation that shelaid for us and aboveall, knowing that shehasgoneon to bewith the Lord.

CHAPTER 1
INTRODUCTION

Ps. 33:1 Rejoice in the Lord, O ye righteous: for praise is comely for the upright.

What does this scripture mean? To praise God is to bestow on Him honour because of His excellence or worth. We should humble ourselves before Him and exalt Him.

Firstly, it is not just a statement, it is a **"command"** to **the righteous/ the 'church'/ the body of Christ.** God's people are commanded to **rejoice in Him.** The psalmist goes on to tell us why we must rejoice; ***"for praise is comely for the upright".*** It's what we are expected to do when you have a relationship with God; when we live uprightly.

Look closely and you will see that rejoicing in the Lord and praising and worshipping Him are synonymous.

However, they are progressive. Giving shouts of praise, thanking Him, lifting up holy hands in surrender to Him, dancing, clapping and being joyful/rejoicing because of who God is; what He has done and what He continues to do. We will never be perfect but sincerity of heart is what the Lord is looking for, from us.

Praising and rejoicing during the times of hardship and suffering ignites faith and trust in God and as we know,

Hebrews 11:6 *But without faith it is impossible to please Him.*

It is emphasised even more in **Ps 147:1** *"Praise ye the Lord: for it is good to sing praises unto our God; for it is pleasant; **and praise is comely".***

It is becoming of us to praise the Lord and more than that it is fitting, pleasant and should be a pleasure because He is worthy. When we have a good relationship with someone, we reflect on their good attributes and we always want to tell them how we feel about them. We also like to tell others about them. We are happy to be in their presence and to build a strong relationship with them.

Well, it is the same way with our relationship with God and even more so because of who He is and what He has done and is doing in our lives. As the relationship grows and we get to the position of "sonship" then it's what He is doing through us. We also should consider who we have become through Him. He is good all the time and all the time He is good. We should be excited to give Him praise.

I must say that praise and worship to God should be the life-style of every believer in Jesus Christ.

As a result, in this book I am dealing primarily with the individual on a one-on-one connection with God, as well as, from the standpoint of the "Praise and Worship" segment during a church service which is being led by a worship leader or worship team.

It is not always easy to praise and worship God when we are experiencing trials and tribulations or during a time of sickness, but the bible says that we should make a sacrifice of praise unto the Lord.

Hebrews 13:15 *By him therefore let us offer the **sacrifice of praise** to God continually, that is, the fruit of our lips giving thanks to his name.*

Now, there is a big difference between singing songs about God, singing praises to Him and worshipping Him. Along with **praise,** comes **thanksgiving** and **rejoicing**; they should go together and may lead to worship. Worship is a higher level; a higher dimension. It's during the worship level that we enter into the **throne-room of God**. Tuck this in your spirit for a minute because we will revisit the throne-room later.

I remember as a child, in Trinidad, my dad took us to a crusade in the savannah when R. W. Schambach was preaching. There was a very large crowd of people and I saw lots of them being healed. There was a lot of clapping, singing and shouting but I did not understand much of what was going on.

However, the first time that I saw inside of a "christian" church I was around 16 years old. We were holidaying in Tobago during the August vacation in the early 1960's and the family was taking a stroll during one evening and passed in front of a "small church" (that's what we called the 'Christian' churches at that time). That was an eye opening experience for me. The congregation was standing, most of them with their hands raised, and they were crying and wailing and shouting but I could not understand what they were saying. It seemed like a whole lot of noise coming from a very sad group of people. I asked myself: "If these people are going to a church where they believed that they were the only ones who are going to heaven to be with the Lord, then why are they so unhappy? Why are they crying like that?" I became very confused and I decided there and then that if being a christian meant that you had to be sad and crying, I did not want to be a part of that. I did not want to be sorrowful.

I grew up Roman Catholic and attended church almost every Sunday. However, in those days there was no praising or clapping or dancing in the Catholic Church. In fact, you could not even speak to the person next to you during 'Mass', which was performed in Latin for the most part and lasted all of half an hour. I did not know much about the bible (because as Catholics we were not allowed to have bibles).

But I learnt from reading my 'catechism book' in the Catholic Church that **God is good** and that **He loves us** and **He sent His Son Jesus to die for us.** So why would I go to church and be sad?

I have been 'born again' or 'saved' since 1981 when I attended a crusade that was organized by a few Pentecostal churches in the North/West district of Trinidad. As a result, I became a member of one of those churches. As I attended that church, I saw people who generally seemed to be happier but, still, some of them had frowns on their faces and some even cried during the time of praise and worship. I still could not understand why, because by this time I had learnt that God loves us unconditionally; He was good all the time; you should rejoice always; you should trust Him; you should thank Him even when there is a problem in your life. (Not thanking Him for the problem but thanking Him in spite of the problem).

Praising God strengthens our faith and reminds us of who God is, the fact that the Holy Spirit is here to teach us and bring us into all truth. Our praise should not be contingent upon how we feel but on who He is and what He has done for us and is still doing. The provisions that He has made for us as His children.

Praising Him during difficult times also brings comfort and joy and peace. There is an anointing that comes when we praise and **worship in *spirit and in truth***. So the question still lingered in my mind: Why the sadness?

Later on, I realized that some christians felt that it was a sin to make a joke or say something funny; to laugh and have fun. I once conducted a bible study at my home and one of the ladies who attended, enquired about whether christians should have fun and make jokes or even smile. She always seemed very sad. Even though she had been a christian for many years. I realized that this idea came about because of the misinterpretation of this passage of scripture.

Matt 12:36 *But I say unto you,* **That every idle word that men shall speak,** *they shall give account thereof in the day of judgment.*

This scripture was referring to the contemptuous words that the Pharisees were speaking against Jesus Christ. Also, we should not be using vile and obscene language.

No thought had been given to the scriptures which tell us to **rejoice in the Lord always;** the **joy of the Lord is my strength;** we should **play musical instruments and sing, dance and make merry in our hearts.**

 Mankind was made with a desire to worship God but when Adam sinned, man became separated from God. However, the desire to worship still remained. So there is a void, a need to worship and man will worship anything or anyone until he becomes born again/regenerated and yielded to the Holy Spirit. Satan even tried to get Jesus Christ to worship him.

Matthew 4:10 *Then saith Jesus unto him, Get thee hence, Satan; for it is written, Thou shalt* **worship the Lord they God,** *and* **Him only shalt thou serve.**

Our Heavenly Father intends for His people to **worship Him and Him only**.

Praise should put a smile on your face, joy in your heart/spirit and a hop in your step. David danced before the Lord with all his might. We should dance like David danced.

2 Sam. 6: 14-16 *14 And David danced before the Lord with all his might; and David was girded with a linen ephod.*

15 So David and all the house of Israel brought up the ark of the Lord with shouting, and with the sound of the trumpet.

16 And as the ark of the Lord came into the city of David, Michal Saul's daughter looked through a window, and saw king David leaping and dancing before the Lord; and she despised him in her heart.

David's wife did not understand, like so many christians today, that, when you have been delivered from some situations that you know if it weren't for God there would have been no way out. Then you do not care who is watching and maybe criticizing you when you get your praise on. David was not naked or dancing vulgar in any way, as some persons believe.

He took off the heavy royal cloak but kept on his ephod and other normal garments and he danced **with all his might V14. He decided that nothing was going to keep him back from rejoicing before the Lord.**

Vs 21 & 22 *And David said unto Michal,* ***It was before the Lord...***

As far as I am concerned praising God is not an option. As christians, praising and worshipping God is what we ought to do. Acknowledging the fact that Jesus died that we could live is enough.

I was under the impression that 'church-going' Christians would at least know how to say 'praise the Lord'. But, I got the shock of my life when I realized that in some churches there was little or no praise and worship. There is what we referred to long ago, back home, as the 'song-service'. But even so, we praised and worshipped during the 'song-service'. In some churches either the songs are not praise or worship songs; some songs are not scriptural; most times the congregation is asked to sit for worship (like a concert with the worship team as performers and the congregation as the audience).

There was this church that I attended where the pastor always referred to the congregation as the audience. Of course, what you say is what you get. The 'audience' sat and listened without as much as a little hint of enthusiasm while the worship team 'performed'.

Frankly, I consider it disrespectful for some persons to be seated while others are trying usher in the presence of God. There should be no spectators (except persons who are ill and cannot stand). but everyone should be involved in worshipping God. In many churches where I visited, the congregation was asked to sit for worship.

While interacting with some of the people, I found out that most of them did not know how to praise God. They just did not know what to say or how to act. They were clueless. I believe that it is the pastor's responsibility to teach the members about praising God and then it's the worship leader's responsibility to lead them in praise and worship into the presence of God.

It really concerns me when I visit churches and find that the members are worshipping the pastor, bishop or whoever the "man/woman of God" is. I have no problem giving honor where honor is due. The pastor should be respected and honored for his submission to God and his/her untiring service to the members of the church and the community. I teach that to those to whom I minister. I have planned pastors' appreciation, pastors' birthday celebrations, I have personally sewn financially into pastors' lives but at no time have I ever replaced God with any of them. It is a very dangerous practice.

However, I have had the horror of witnessing (both in Trinidad and in the United States) where the pastor is praised, worshipped, preached about, referred to as "the king that God gave to us", and the list goes on. I dare to say that it seems to me that some of those pastors enjoy the homage paid to them in God's stead, and sad to say, are allowing what started out as ministries or churches to become cults. I am fully aware that mankind needs to be appreciated and rewarded and observed for his/her accomplishments, hard work and the like but God should still be seen as the One who made it possible. Ultimately, God alone deserves all the praise, all the honour and all the glory. We have to remember who God is. He is the one, true and living God. He is our provider, miracle worker, Waymaker, the King of kings and Lord of lords. He is Omnipotent, Omnipresent and Omniscient.

CHAPTER 2
WHO HAS THAT AWESOME PRIVILEGE?

WHO'S awesome privilege is it to praise the Lord? It is indeed a privilege, but even more than that it is a responsibility.

I speak about responsibility because we, as christians, are commanded or exhorted to praise God because *"praise is comely for the upright" Ps.33:1 (b).* Everything and everyone that has breath should praise the Lord.

Ps. 150:6

Let *everything that hath breath* praise the Lord. Praise ye the Lord.

When we, as Christians, think about the Lord and what He has done for us and who we are in Him, we should just become overwhelmed with emotion. *Selah/Think about it.*

Isaiah 53:3-12

He is **despised and rejected of men; a man of sorrows, and acquainted with grief**: and we hid as it were our faces from Him; **He was despised,** and we esteemed Him not. Surely **He hath borne our griefs,** and **carried our sorrows**: yet we did esteem Him **stricken, smitten of God, and afflicted**. But **He was wounded for our transgressions, He was bruised for our iniquities: the chastisement of our peace was upon Him; and with His stripes we are healed.** All we like sheep have gone astray; we have turned every one to his own way; and the **Lord hath laid on Him the iniquity of us all. He was oppressed, and He was afflicted,** yet He opened not His mouth: He is brought as a lamb to the slaughter, and as a sheep before her shearers is dumb, so He openeth not His mouth. He was taken from prison and from judgment: and who shall declare His generation? for He was cut off out of the land of the living: for the transgression of my people was He stricken. And He made His grave with the wicked, and with the rich in His death; because **He had done no violence, neither was any deceit in His mouth**. Yet it pleased the Lord to **bruise Him**; He hath **put Him to grief**: when thou shalt make His soul an offering for sin, He shall see His seed, He shall prolong His days, and the pleasure of the Lord shall prosper in His hand. He shall see of the travail of His soul, and shall be satisfied: by His knowledge shall my righteous servant justify many; for He shall bear their iniquities.

Therefore will I divide Him a portion with the great, and He shall divide the spoil with the strong; because He hath poured out His soul unto death: and He was numbered with the transgressors; and **He bare the sin of many, and made intercession for the transgressors.**

In this passage of scripture the prophet Isaiah is prophesying about the sufferings of Jesus Christ who had not been born as yet, and therefore had not gone through those things.

I pray that all believers will become excited, grateful and enthusiastic about Jesus' sacrifice on the cross for us and as a result, will give Him all the praise; and all the honour; and all the glory and the adoration that is due to Him. Even more than being our responsibility, it is an honour and a privilege to be allowed by God to enter into His presence, to stand before the King of Kings and Lord of Lords. In addition to what He suffered, He is seated at the right hand of the Father making intercession for us.

Ps. 100 1 - 2, 4 - 5 1 Make a joyful noise unto the Lord, all ye lands. 2 *Serve the Lord with* **gladness***: come before his presence with* **singing. 4 Enter into His gates with thanksgiving, and into His courts with praise: be thankful unto Him , and bless His name. 5 For the Lord is good; His mercy is everlasting; and His truth endureth to all generations.**

The psalmist is calling on all the inhabitants of the earth to be grateful and joyful and to make merry; to shout and sing and give God praise and thanks. Why? Because He is good, He is merciful and He is faithful to all generations. Most unsaved people say "praise God" without even really thinking about Him. Some, even christians, say: "praise the man above" or "the man upstairs" which, to me, shows their ignorance. I believe if they knew better they would do better. Firstly, He is not a man. He came to earth as a man and paid the ransom for us with His life. But He is the second person in the Godhead.

1 John 5:7 *"For there are three that bear record in heaven, the Father, the Word and the Holy Ghost and these three are one."*

For those who may not know, Jesus is the Word. ***John 1:14*** *"The Word was made flesh and dwelt among us."*

Ps. 67:3 *Let the people praise thee, O God;* ***let all the people praise thee***.

The time will come when all the nations of the earth will be occupied with the people of God who will be praising and worshipping Him continuously. During that time when we will return to the earth to rule and reign with Jesus for one thousand years.

In the meantime, we are to occupy till He comes.

1 Peter 2:9 *But ye are a chosen generation, a royal priesthood,* **an holy nation,** *a peculiar people; that* **ye should shew forth the praises of him who hath called you out of darkness into his marvellous light;**

As the holy nation, the called-out ones, we should be excited to show forth His praises.

Angels

Christians are not the only ones with the responsibility to praise and worship God. Even the **angels in heaven are continuously praising and exalting God**.

There is plenty of evidence as seen both in the Old and New Testaments.

Rev. 7:11 *And all* **the angels** *stood round about the throne, and about the elders and the four beasts, and fell before the throne on their faces, and* **worshipped God**.

Hebrews 1:6 *And again, when he bringeth in the first begotten into the world, he saith,* **And let all the angels of God worship him.**

Ps. 103:20-22 *Bless the Lord,* **ye His angels**, *that excel in strength, that do His commandments, hearkening unto the voice of His word.*

Bless ye the Lord, all ye His hosts*; ye ministers of His,* that do His pleasure. ***Bless the Lord****,* all His works in all places of His dominion: bless the Lord, O my soul.

Isaiah 6:1-3 *In the year that King Uzziah died I saw also the Lord sitting upon a throne, high and lifted up, and his train filled the temple. Above it stood* **the seraphims:** *each one had six wings; with twain he covered his face, and with twain he covered his feet, and with twain he did fly.* **And one cried unto another,** *and said,* **Holy, holy, holy, is the Lord of hosts: the whole earth is full of His glory.**

Luke 2:13 - 14 *And suddenly there was with* **the angel a multitude of the heavenly host praising God, and saying, Glory to God in the highest***, and on earth peace, good will toward men.*

CHAPTER 3
WHY WE SHOULD PRAISE GOD

God deserves our praise, but He doesn't need our praise. He exists of himself. There is nothing that we can do that would change Him.

Those of us who love and serve Him should consider it a privilege to praise and worship God. Our praise to Him benefits us in more ways than we can imagine.

When our praise and worship become a lifestyle and we praise God sincerely, we secure a kingdom connection and our spirits are transformed because our minds are renewed and we dwell in the spiritual realm.

Rom. 12:2 *Do not be conformed to this world but be transformed by the renewing of your mind.*

We are to be spiritually minded. We are in the world but not of the world we are of the spirit, the Holy Spirit. Our minds are renewed by reading and studying the word of God and ultimately living the word. A very important aspect of renewing our minds is spending quality, quiet time with the Lord. Unfortunately, this is something that many christians neglect to do.

Sincere praise and worship ought to put a hunger and thirst in our spirits for more of God; to know Him more and to become more like Jesus. We belong to the kingdom of God and should be kingdom minded. It also helps us to develop a personal relationship with God where we talk with Him and listen to Him talk back to us. Prayer is a 2-way communication.

The bible, our handbook for victorious living, tells us clearly in so many instances **why** praising and thanking God is beneficial to us.

Let us take a look:

Ps. 103:1-5 *Bless the Lord, O my soul: and all that is within me,* **bless His holy name.**

Bless the Lord, O my soul, **and forget not all His benefits;** *Who* **forgiveth all thine iniquities**; *who* **healeth all thy diseases;** *Who* **redeemeth thy life from destruction;** *who* **crowneth thee with lovingkindness and tender mercies;** *Who* **satisfieth thy mouth with good things;** *so that* **thy youth is renewed like the eagle's.**

Those are very good reasons to give Him some resounding praise. Are you still not convinced **why** we need to give God praise and worship? Let's examine those verses more closely. The psalmist is exhorting himself here when he says **bless the Lord, O my soul and all that is within me, bless His holy name.** He desires to bless the Lord with his spirit, soul (mind, will and emotions) and body.

His entire being is to be involved in the act of praising and worshipping God. His body - posture: standing, bowing, kneeling, dancing; speaking, singing, clapping; His soul - an act of his will, his decision, with intelligence and purpose. His spirit - from his inner man; a place of repentance, sacrifice and love for God.

He then reminds himself of **all the benefits** that the Lord bestows upon those who are His own and who diligently seek Him.

Now he names some of the benefits. He counted his many blessings one by one.

v3 'Who forgiveth all thine iniquities' - he remembers the sacrifice of Jesus when He went to the cross, He shed His blood and paid the price for his sins. Jesus died so that our sins may be forgiven.

v3 (b) Who healeth all thy diseases; not only did Jesus Christ die to forgive us our sins but also to heal all diseases and sicknesses and to deliver us from every plan of the devil.

v4 'He redeemeth thy life from destruction.' Yet another reason that David remembers to praise God. I feel he thinks about the time when Saul pursued after him to destroy him and God delivered him. Was there a time in your life when things seemed to be heading downhill fast?

Problems on every side - marriage falling apart, financial difficulties, homelessness, sickness, children going astray and anything the devil decides to throw at you. Until suddenly or maybe a little at a time burdens are lifted, problems solved and you know that you know that it could only be God.

v4(b) 'Who crowneth thee with loving kindness and tender mercies.' David left nothing out. He did not take anything for granted and we should not either. Just by being God's children His grace and mercy are extended to us.

His blessings and mercies are new every morning. As we awake each morning we should be thankful for the breath of life; thankful for health and strength in our bodies and soundness of mind; thank Him for the very air that we breathe. He is Jehovah Nissi - our banner, our protector, our shield and buckler, and His banner over us is love. He loves us unconditionally. So, even when we sin as christians, He is still there waiting for us to ask Him for forgiveness because *He is faithful and just to forgive us and cleanse us from all unrighteousness* **1 John 1:9.**

v5 'Who satisfieth thy mouth with good things; so that thy youth is renewed like the eagle's.' When we rejoice in the Lord and we find happiness in praising Him our physical bodies as well as our spirits are strengthened. The word says that the 'joy of the Lord is our strength'.

We are able to soar above our problems and we are strengthened in our bodies, souls and spirits. We are triune beings so God is concerned about every aspect of our well being. We will also enjoy stress-free living. We need to put ourselves in the same mindset as the psalmist David when he wrote Psalm 103.

This would be an appropriate time to remember and thank Him for all His goodness towards us as individuals, as well as families, districts, and nations, and all the benefits that He has provided for us, His children. We are all His creation, but only those of us who are saved are His children. The benefits of being children of the Most High King are numerous.

In **v2** we remember **all his benefits**. Not only our material needs and wants but also His protection, His guidance, His comfort, His peace, His grace, He's always present; (He promised never to leave nor forsake us. He is Jehovah Shammah, the ever present God).

Some people were in deep trouble with the law of the land or even with their neighbors, others in general. Once we have received Christ as Savior we are justified by his grace, which is unmerited favor. All of past sins are forgiven and Jesus Christ has taken the punishment in our place so we are justified.

However, we may still have to stand trial and face the judge but I guarantee you that if you surrender your life to praise and worship, your atmosphere and your perspective on life will shift; you will be able to trust God more. Not only will you experience the forgiveness of God but sometimes also forgiveness from man.

Acts 13:39 *And by him all that believe are justified from all things, from which ye could not be justified by the law of Moses.*

The deepest level of worship is praising God in spite of the physical and mental pain, thanking God during the trials, trusting Him when we are tempted to lose hope and loving Him when He seems so distant and far away.

Even before I came to know Christ, before becoming 'born again', I remember going through some intense struggles in my marriage and I was crying out to God. I said to Him, "God I am willing to take this punishment for my sins because Jesus went through so much for me when He shed His blood for the sins of the world but Lord I did not kill anyone so why do I have to suffer like this? Of course, being Roman Catholic I was taught that we had to do penance for our sins.

However, now even during direct attacks of the enemy I know who my God is, who I am in Him, the authority I have over the enemy and I know the strategies of the enemy.

So when he strikes, I recognize him, I deal with him and I praise God in the midst of the trials. I appropriate the joy of the Lord because therein lies my strength.

Mankind is born with an innate desire to worship. There is a void in man's spirit, a longing to worship and the Holy Spirit is ready and waiting to fill that void, for our benefit. It is only God who can satisfy that longing. However, some people worship other people and some worship things, e.g. spouses, children, homes/houses, animals, jobs, trees, the sun and moon, statues etc. Anything or anyone that is worshipped in the place of the one true and living God becomes an idol. Every believer knows and has experienced the goodness of God. If we examine **Psalm 107,** we will see that everytime the children of Israel disobeyed God they got into distress. Then they cried out to the Lord who heard them and delivered them. The key verses in that psalm are **vs. 8, 15, 21 & 31** and they all read the same:

Ps. 107 : 8, 15, 21 & 31

*Oh that men would **praise the Lord** for **His goodness**, and for **His wonderful works** to the children of men!.*

Praise increases our faith in God. It changes the atmosphere from doubt to faith when we remember who He is; His promises; what He has done for us in the past; and then we know that we can trust Him with the future.

He is the same yesterday, today and forever. So what He has done before He can do it again and then some. With Him nothing is impossible. He is the God of possibilities and miracles. Also, with the shift in the atmosphere and increased faith, the anointing flows and releases healing, deliverance, and power. In the midst of our challenges and the storms of life we ought to **praise Him for His goodness** and **His wonderful works**.

As christians, we ought to remember. Even if we think that God has not done anything for us personally, we should think again. Who has made us and is keeping us alive? We are fearfully and wonderfully made **Ps.139:14.** Read the Word and learn about all the promises He has made to us and know that He keeps them. He is not a man that He should lie. Learn of Him and His love and his goodness towards His children, the redeemed.

We can go all the way back before Jesus came to the earth as a man. Remember when God parted the Red Sea for the children of Israel? ***Exodus 12:34 to 15:21*** Let's think about it for a moment. It was after all the pleading and plagues that Pharaoh finally said yes to Moses to "Let my people go". However, he still changed his mind and he and his army pursued after them. They were supernaturally led by the pillar of cloud by day and the pillar of fire by night. There was the Red Sea in front of them and Pharaoh's army behind; on both sides were mountains and that was the route which Moses decided to take or so the Israelites thought.

Obviously, he was led by the Lord to pass that way. What a situation for these people. But you know what? God showed up and showed himself strong. He made a way where there was no way. He is the **Waymaker.** He opened the Red Sea for His people to walk through and then He closed it up on the Egyptians. Moses and the children of Israel sang a song of **praise and thanksgiving to God** for His goodness towards them.

*Matt 14:14 - 21 And **Jesus** went forth, and saw a great multitude, and **was moved with compassion** toward them, and **He healed their sick**. And when it was evening, His disciples came to Him, saying, This is a desert place, and the time is now past; send the multitude away, that they may go into the villages, and buy themselves victuals. But Jesus said unto them, **They need not depart; give ye them to eat**. And they say unto Him, We have here but five loaves, and two fishes. He said, Bring them hither to me. And He commanded the multitude to sit down on the grass, and took the five loaves, and the two fishes, and looking up to heaven, He blessed, and brake, and gave the loaves to His disciples, and the disciples to the multitude. And they did all eat, and were filled: and they took up of the fragments that remained twelve baskets full. And they that had eaten were about five thousand men, beside women and children.*

He is a **God of compassion; a God who heals; a God of miracles;** the disciples collected twelve baskets full of leftovers. He is **a God of more than enough**. Reasons to give Him praise and thanks.

Not to mention what Jesus has done for you and I. He shed His blood and paid the price for our sins and much more than that.

1 Peter 2:24 *Who his own self **bare our sins in his own body on the tree,** that we, being dead to sins, should live unto righteousness: by whose stripes ye were healed.*

Isaiah 53:5 *He was **wounded for our transgressions,** He was **bruised for our iniquities:** the **chastisement of our peace was upon Him**; and **by His stripes we were healed.***

In fact, just read the whole chapter and also read **Matt 27** and be familiar with the sufferings of Jesus at the time of His crucifixion. Also, we should think about where He is now in relation to us and where we are in relation to Him. Let's picture our lives before knowing Jesus Christ. Could you imagine where you were heading? Where are you now? Who are you now? You are a brand new person in Christ because of His sacrifice for you.

2 Cor. 5:17 *Therefore if any man be in Christ, he is a new creature: old things are passed away; behold all things are become new.*

Salvation is the biggest miracle of all time and we should be constantly thanking God for that gift.

Eph. 2:8 & 9 *For by **grace are ye saved through faith**; and that not of yourselves: it is the **gift of God**: Not of works, lest any man should boast.*

We know that if it were not for God our lives would have been in such a mess, **but God. Glory be to God! Give Him praise! Hallelujah!**

Another example of **Jesus' compassion and healing:**

Lk 18 : 41 - 43 *Saying,* **What wilt thou that I should do unto thee?** *And he said, Lord, that I may receive my sight. And Jesus said unto him,* **Receive thy sight; thy faith has saved thee.** *And immediately he received his sight, and followed him,* **glorifying God:** *and* **all the people,** *when they saw it,* **gave praise unto God.**

In **Matt 20** the account of this incident says that there were two blind men and in **vs34** he says *that* **Jesus had compassion on them**, *and touched their eyes:* He is a **God of love, compassion, mercy and grace**; a **God of miracles.**

It doesn't matter what is taking place in our lives at this present time, the devil is already defeated. Jesus destroyed satan over 2000 years ago, when He shed His blood for us, went to the grave, took the keys of death, hell and the grave from him. Then He arose triumphantly and gave us, the church, the keys of the kingdom of heaven. If this does not excite the believer and give a reason to praise Him, I do not know what will.

Ps. 100 : 5 *For the* **Lord is good; his mercy is everlasting**; *and* **his truth** *endureth to all generations.*

There is Power in Praise

Exousia power is the authority to bind and loose; to decree a thing and it shall be established unto thee:

Job 22:28 *Thou shalt also decree a thing, and it shall be established unto thee: and the light shall shine upon thy ways.*

Sincere praise and worship can calm the storms in our lives and break the chains that bind us.

Acts 16 : 22 - 26** And the multitude rose up together against them: and the magistrates **rent off their clothes,** and commanded to **beat them.** And when they had laid **many stripes upon them,** they cast them into prison, charging the jailor to keep them safely: Who, having received such a charge, **thrust them into the inner prison**, and made their **feet fast in the stocks**. And at midnight Paul and Silas **prayed, and sang praises unto God:** and **the prisoners heard them**. And **suddenly** there was a **great earthquake,** so that the **foundations of the prison were shaken:** and immediately all the **doors were opened**, and **every one's bands were loosed.

Notice that **Paul and Silas did not have a pity party, nor did they enjoy a quiet, dignified evening of praying and singing praises softly unto God.** The bible says that the prisoners heard them and suddenly there was a great earthquake; the foundations of the prison were shaken; the doors were opened; and the prisoners' bands were loosed.

Let us try to picture this scenario. Paul and Silas obviously made some extra loud noises unto the Lord. So much so that although they were in the inner prison all the other prisoners heard them.

Acts 16 : 30 - 34 In ***v 30 (b)*** the keeper of the prison said to Paul and Silas: *Sirs,* ***what must I do to be saved***? At the end of the day his household was **saved**, **baptised** and **they rejoiced.** Normally, we think about the miracle of the prison doors being opened, but very little, if any, thought is given to the **miracle of salvation** of an entire family as a result of two persons praising God. That's a great example of **the power in praise. Effectual fervent praise** can cause breakthroughs in our personal lives, families, churches and in our sphere of influence.

James 5 : 16 (b) *The effectual fervent* ***prayer*** *of a righteous man availeth much.*

Be aware that praying is communicating with God and praising is one form of praying.

Shackles may fall, chains break, walls tumble down, satan's strongholds broken, generational curses broken, evil words and incantations reversed, strengthening our relationship with God and so much more.

Praise is a weapon of war!!!

There is war in the heavenlies. We know that we are in a spiritual war. The war of God against Satan; of good against evil; and we are either on God's side or the devil's side. There is no middle ground.

PRAISE changes our attitude and the atmosphere around us. When we begin to praise God, the demons tremble. *I am talking about deep heartfelt praise and worship.*

Eph. 6:12 *For we **wrestle not against flesh and blood**, but against principalities, against powers, against the rulers of the darkness of this world, against spiritual wickedness in high places.*

Praise is an integral part of our warfare against the enemy. The word wrestle means to fight, to afflict blows on our opponent. Only in this case, they are spirits, evil spirits. Most of the battles are fought in our minds where we are tempted to do wrong or not to do right. Praise helps us to focus on God and His attributes and to have better communication with Him, thus hearing Him speak to us and give us direction.

In this next Psalm it is assumed that David wrote it during the time that he was being pursued by Absalom. He decided to give God a sacrifice of praise in advance of the victory.

Ps. 27 : 6 *And now my head **will be lifted up above my enemies around me**; and I will offer in His tent **sacrifices with shouts of joy;** I will sing, yes, **I will sing praises to the Lord.***

Another great example of **praise as a weapon of war** is when King Jehoshaphat was told that the enemies of Judah and Jerusalem were setting an ambush against them. He called a solemn assembly and fasted and worshipped God. The Lord sent His word of encouragement through Jahaziel, the son of Zechariah, saying unto them: "Be not afraid nor dismayed by reason of this great multitude; for the battle is not yours, but God's". Jehoshaphat continued to encourage his people in **praise and worship to God** and he was directed by God how he should line up his army. The rest is history.

2 Chron. 20 : 15, 21 - 22 *And he said, Hearken ye, all Judah, and ye inhabitants of Jerusalem, and thou king Jehoshaphat, Thus saith the Lord unto you, Be not afraid nor dismayed by reason of this great multitude; **for the battle is not yours, but God's.***

*And when he had consulted with the people, he appointed singers unto the Lord, and that should praise the beauty of holiness, as they went out before the army, and to say, Praise the Lord; for his mercy endureth for ever. And **when they began to sing and to praise, the Lord set ambushments against the children of Ammon, Moab, and mount Seir, which were come against Judah; and they were smitten.***

When we decide to praise God in spite of impending danger and even during the time of battle, we give Him the permission to take over and we can confidently say "the battle is not mine but God's".

Josh 6: 15 & 16** And it came to pass on the seventh day, that they rose early about the dawning of the day, and compassed the city after the same manner seven times: only on that day they compassed the city seven times. And it came to pass at the seventh time, **when the priests blew with the trumpets, Joshua said unto the people, Shout; for the Lord hath given you the city.

In this scenario, Joshua and the mighty men of war were charged by God to take down the **walls of Jericho**. Joshua got instructions from the Lord who outlined the order of the procession. The armed men of war led the way followed by the seven priests with their trumpets made of rams' horns which were called 'horns of jubilee', then the Ark of the Lord. We must picture this scene where the armed men of war had no cause to use their weapons. Instead, everyday the priests blew the horns of jubilee which was the sound of praise and on the seventh day Joshua gave the command to the people to **SHOUT for the Lord had given them the city**. I believe that it is safe to assume that this was no ordinary shout. It was a shout of **thanksgiving, praise and worship**. A resounding **shout of VICTORY!!!** A praise that was full of **faith.**

2 Cor. 10:4 *The weapons of our warfare are not carnal but mighty through God to the pulling down of strongholds.*

Since the battles are spiritual then the weapons have to be spiritual as well. We have power/authority over the enemy to pull down those strongholds/thoughts that he puts in our minds; to break chains that bind us; to break down walls that have been erected to block the plan of God for our lives.

Matt 18:18 *Verily I say unto you, whatsoever ye shall bind on earth shall be bound in heaven: and whatsoever ye shall loose on earth shall be loosed in heaven.*

1 Sam 16:18, 23 18 *Then answered one of the servants, and said, Behold, I have seen a **son of Jesse** the Bethlehemite, that is **cunning in playing,** and a **mighty valiant man**, and **a man of war,** and **prudent in matters,** and **a comely person,** and **the Lord is with him.***

23 *And it came to pass, when the evil spirit from God was upon Saul, that David took an harp, and played with his hand: so Saul was refreshed, and was well, and the evil spirit departed from him.*

Now, the David whom I have come to know through reading the book of Psalms would hardly play a musical instrument without composing a song of praise and thanksgiving.

Therefore, I think that it is safe to say that when David praised and worshipped God, Saul was delivered.

Demons tremble and cannot stand it when we praise the Lord, especially, in spite of our circumstances. Imagine satan is coming against you with sickness, financial lack/difficulties, relationship issues and everything else he could find to bring you stress and you do not know where to turn. But, instead of pulling your hair out, you begin to praise the Lord. OMG!!! Satan and/or his imps will have no choice but to take their leave. We have to be steadfast with our praise and thanksgiving.

CHAPTER 4
WHEN SHOULD WE BE PRAISING GOD?

When is the appropriate time to praise God? Is it in the morning, noon time or evening. Maybe on a special day of the week is best. Better still during a particular season, like Resurrection Sunday, Christmas Day or Pentecost Sunday. What about when your birthday comes around; the purchase of a new car; built or bought a house; won the lottery. These are all really good times to show your gratitude and to praise and worship God.

*Ps. 104:33 I will sing unto the Lord **as long as I live**: I will sing praise to my God while I have my being.*

*Phil. 4:4 **Rejoice** in the Lord **alway**: and again I say, **Rejoice**.*

*Ps. 113:3 From the **rising of the sun** unto the **going down of the same**, the Lord's name is to be praised.*

Praise Him in the morning, praise Him in the noontime, praise Him in the going down of the day. He should be praised every day, all day, 24/7.

As soon as I open my eyes in the morning I say: "Good morning Father, good morning Jesus, good morning Holy Spirit. Thank you for the dawning of a brand new day. This is the day that you have made. I will rejoice and be glad in it. Thank you for a sound mind and a healthy body. I will praise You, Lord, in the morning; praise You in the noon time, praise You at the going down of the day. Hallelujah!!!!! Glory be to God!!!!! Then I go on from there.

Worship as a lifestyle

It is not necessary to have music to praise or worship God because as a matter of fact as children of God we should live a **lifestyle of worship.** Praise should always be in our mouths and in our thoughts. Even during the performance of our duties, whether it's a job or profession, we should always work as unto God and He deserves our best. Therefore, we should be some of the best workers in the workplace. We should exhibit efficiency, effectiveness, patience, kindness, wisdom and happiness even when we are treated harshly or unfairly. When doing menial tasks at home or at work. It may be washing, cleaning the toilet, gardening, painting, whatever duty calls us to do.

I cannot say this enough, praise should always be on our lips and in our hearts.

Luke 6:45 *A good man out of the good treasure of his heart bringeth forth that which is good; and an evil man out of the evil treasure of his heart bringeth forth that which is evil: for of the abundance of the heart his mouth speaketh.*

If, as christians, we enjoy the peace of God in our lives and we think good thoughts and experience the joy of the Lord, in spite of the negative circumstances that may surround us then it is inevitable that we will always be praising God.

All day long with customers – while you are dealing with customers whether you work in retail, corporate or you are a professional you should never be ashamed to acknowledge God. While attending a business meeting and something happens that is obviously the work of God, let it be known by you saying praise the Lord or glory be to God. We are to acknowledge Him in all our ways and He will direct our paths. Not only that but we should not be ashamed to let people know that we love God and have a relationship with Him. Praise and worship should be the lifestyle of every believer.

When praising God sincerely the anointing will flow and there may be a transference of spirit, the Holy Spirit, and the other person especially if he/she is a believer may begin to praise God also. Just the very presence of God ought to bring peace and change our demeanor from sad to happy/glad; from despair to encouragement/hope.

As in the case of Paul and Silas in the prison the jailor and his family received their salvation.

Let your light shine and give God the glory and praise for what He has done. Praise Him in the good times or even during the times when we're experiencing trials and tribulations. In fact, when we don't feel like praising Him, it is the best time to do so.

Heb. 13:15 *By him therefore let us offer the **sacrifice of praise to God continually,** that is, the fruit of our lips giving thanks to his name.*

Sometimes it really calls for a sacrifice. After a hard day's work, you might be frustrated, tired, no money to pay your bills and the hungry children looking at you to be fed. You have to push hard and force yourself to give Him praise because praise will change the atmosphere. There will be a shift because God dwells in the praises of His people. Miracles will take place and we will experience answers to our prayers.

While at home working around the house: cooking, cleaning the toilet, gardening, walking the dog, exercising – at the gym. "At all times" means exactly what it says: **At all times**.

Ps.34:1 *I will bless the Lord **at all times**: his praise shall **continually** be in my mouth.*

The deepest level of worship is praising God in spite of the pain, thanking Him during the trials and tribulation, trusting Him when we are tempted to lose hope and loving Him when He seems so distant and far away.

The bible says that we are to encourage ourselves in the Lord. Well I have found that the best way to do that is to praise Him. Once we begin to praise God we remember how good He is to us, all the time, and the obvious thing would be to thank Him for what He has done, what He is doing and blessings on the way.

This should lead us to His attributes, His promises, His greatness, Who He is to us and who we are in Him.

What it all boils down to, is **Faith,** without which it is impossible to please God. When we trust God and the integrity of His Word then we cannot help but praise Him during the storm because:

Romans 8:28 *"And we know that all things work together for good to them that love God, to them who are called according to His purpose".*

Then instead of focusing on the situation at hand, we can believe/have faith for the results. Of course, praise and thanks will soothe the hurts and disappointments and we will be encouraged in the Lord.

Many churches miss out on a crucial time when corporate thanksgiving and praise should be given to the Lord. After singing a song or chorus about God and His goodness, the congregation should be allowed to praise and thank Him for His goodness in their own lives and in so doing, they will develop their own style of worship to God. e.g. **We are singing 'great is the Lord and greatly to be praised.'** But what happens is that they go from one song about Him to the next and no real praise is given to Him.

CHAPTER 5
WHERE SHOULD WE PRAISE GOD?

Now that we are aware of the reasons for praising God, it is reasonable to enquire **where** we should praise Him. Maybe the question should be: "Where shouldn't we praise the Lord?" The Bible, the Word of God, the manual for living has the answer for every question we may have about life and living. This question is no exception.

Let's see what **Jesus,** Himself, had to say about this matter when He spoke with the Samaritan woman at the well.

John 4:20-24 *20 Our fathers worshipped in this mountain; and ye say, that in Jerusalem is the place where men ought to worship.*

21 ***Jesus saith unto her,*** *Woman, believe me, the hour cometh, when ye shall* ***neither in this mountain, nor yet at Jerusalem,*** *worship the Father.*

22 Ye worship ye know not what: we know what we worship: for salvation is of the Jews.

23 *But the hour cometh, and now is, when* **the true worshippers shall worship the Father** <u>**in spirit and in truth**</u>**: for the Father seeketh such to worship him.**

24 God is a Spirit: and they that worship him must worship him <u>**in spirit and in truth.**</u>

The woman was concerned about where to worship. She remembered that in times past her forefathers worshipped in this mountain while the Jews claimed that Jerusalem was the place where men ought to worship. Could you imagine if everyone from everywhere had to travel to Jerusalem to worship God?

God is not concerned about **where** but **how we worship Him. We must worship Him in spirit and in truth.**

Back in 2015 or 2016, I was visiting a group of elderly Christians who were meeting at the home of the group's leader, for one evening per week for about two hours. This was a cell group, if you will. I was checking out this group to decide whether they were a good fit for me to join them.

The format was the same every time they met. The leader of the group would pray the opening prayer and then she would read the scripture from a daily devotional and give an explanation; the group sang a couple of choruses while remaining seated.

After which the leader alone gave God a little praise and closed in prayer. Then it was time to eat. We enjoyed the food and fellowship, which was the most interactive part of the evening. After visiting for two or three weeks, one evening I suggested that maybe we can all join in the "praise" aspect of the "service". I was met with such negative responses I could not believe it. The excuses varied but the one that blew my mind the most was the woman who said that she praised God at her home but did not like to praise Him in the presence of other people. In other words, she was ashamed or embarrassed to praise God for other people to hear. The saddest part was that the group leader gave in to them instead of teaching them, well, I suppose she could not teach what she did not know. I wondered whether their bibles were different from mine because my bible says that I should praise Him in the congregation of the people.

Psalm 107:32 *Let them exalt him in the **congregation of the people**, and **praise Him in the assembly of the elders.***

We should not be ashamed to praise God publicly and tell others of His goodness. We should always be ready with a testimony of who God is, what He has done and our love for Him. It is important also to remind others of what the 'word' says. In so doing we are reminding them of who God is. Acknowledge what He has done and give Him praise and thanks in the midst of the unsaved. Whether it is at work, out shopping, on the bus, plane or train, we ought to testify of His goodness towards us.

Ps. 150:1 (a)** Praise ye the Lord. **Praise God in His sanctuary:

We should praise and worship our Lord and Saviour anywhere and everywhere. Especially among our brothers and sisters in Christ.

***Psalm 34:1** I will bless the Lord **at all times** his praise shall continually be in my mouth.*

It matters not where I am or even what time of day. I will bless the Lord at all times. So wherever I am, I will bless the Lord. If I'm before a king, if I'm before the judge, it does not matter. If I'm at work or if I'm at play, I will praise the Lord!

Shortly after I gave my life to the Lord (became born-again or got saved however you want to say it) I read in the bible where Jesus asked his disciples to spend one hour with him to pray. At that time I awoke at 5 a.m. to get ready for work which was a long way from home. I decided that I had to spend 1 hour with the Lord before getting ready, so I woke at 4 am in order to spend the first hour with the Lord before leaving home for work at 6:30am. It was not long before I was sent even further away to work and I could not wake any earlier than 4 am. So I did my praise and worship and prayer and quiet time and everything while on the road in my car. I experienced the most glorious encounters with my Heavenly Father during that period.

My car became one of my favorite places to praise and worship my God. A huge part of that time was spent rejoicing and singing and dancing, yes dancing while driving, in his presence. In fact, I believe that it was during those sessions in my car that I developed and refined my praise. Even before this period, as soon as I entered my car to go anywhere I got into praise mode. It did not matter whether I was alone or had company or even where I was heading. Only now, on my long journey to work, it was more intense because it became an extension and indeed an integral part of my early morning devotion.

Ps. 100:4 *Enter into **His gates** with Thanksgiving, and into **His courts** with praise: be thankful unto Him, and bless His name.*

His gates and His courts are metaphors since there are no physical gates nor physical courts in heaven. In fact, He is omnipresent meaning that He is everywhere at the same time. So that, 'entering into His gates and His courts' is being in His presence. We are to enter into His presence with praise and thanksgiving. It's a call to worship, a call to praise and a call to give thanks to our God. Our praise opens the gates that allow us to enter into His presence.

CHAPTER 6
HOW OUGHT WE TO PRAISE/WORSHIP GOD?

In most instances when the Lord asks us to do something He indicates to us exactly how it should be done. Most times He gives direction step by step, not all at once. It's the same when the Holy Spirit is teaching us to praise and worship God. If we have a desire to worship God and we seek the Holy Spirit for direction He *will* teach us.

I know that some of you may be wondering why I sometimes say God and other times I refer to the Holy Spirit. Well let me set the record straight. The God-Head includes three persons, the Father, the Son and the Holy Spirit/Holy Ghost. Three distinct persons but one God. Yes it is a mystery, but it is scriptural. Check **1 John 5:7** *For there are three that bear record in heaven,* **the Father, the Word, and the Holy Ghost: and these three are one.** I am assuming that we all know that the 'Word' is Jesus Christ, the Son *who was made flesh and dwelt amongst us,* according to the scriptures.

In Spirit And In Truth

In **John 4:21-24** Jesus reveals to the Samaritan woman that it's not **where** we worship Him that matters but **how**. In the early days the Jews went up to Mount Gerizim or to the synagogue at Jerusalem but Jesus said to her **v23** *But the hour cometh, and now is, when the true worshippers shall worship the Father in spirit and in truth: for the Father seeketh such to worship Him. God is a Spirit: and they that worship Him must worship Him **in spirit and in truth.***

Worshipping in spirit and in truth means that it must come from the heart. Not our physical hearts but deep down in our spirits. It must come from a place of repentance, submission, thankfulness, gratefulness and in keeping with the truth of God's revealed word.

Besides the condition of our hearts, the scriptures also tell us in no uncertain terms **how** we should behave when praising God.

For example, **Ps. 47:1 O Clap your hands**, *all ye people;* **shout unto God** *with the voice of triumph.*

Clearly, we are told to **clap and shout** unto God. One may ask, is God deaf that we have to shout? No, God is not deaf. Our praise does not affect Him one way or the other. He is God and He changes not. However, when we pray with faith, we believe that God will answer us and grant our petitions, then we should be enthusiastic in our praise.

Not only should we shout but **shout with the voice of triumph,** sometimes even before obtaining an answer to our prayer/petition, by faith we know that we are victorious in Christ.

We are to open our mouths and shout. Get radical in our praise because He deserves it. Listen to the instructions of the Holy Spirit while you worship Him. During worship He will direct you as to what He desires of you. You may feel to lift your hands; He may require you to kneel where you are or at the altar; He may even desire for you to prostrate yourself before Him. We just have to be sensitive to the leading of the Holy Spirit and be obedient.

Phil. 4:4 Rejoice in the Lord always and again I say rejoice.

Isaiah 61:3 To appoint unto them that mourn in Zion, to give unto them beauty for ashes, the oil of joy for mourning, **the garment of praise for the spirit of heaviness;** that they might be called trees of righteousness, the planting of the Lord, that he might be glorified.

The prophet Isaiah was prophesying about the time when Jesus would come and make the ultimate sacrifice for us so that we may enjoy abundant life. When we would experience joy instead of mourning; beauty for ashes; praise and thanksgiving instead of murmuring and sadness.

As God's people we should not be sad, in fear, in depression and forlorn. Although negative situations may come our way, we have to encourage ourselves in the Lord, put on our garment of praise for the spirit of heaviness and shame the devil.

One of my pet peeves is when pastors and worship leaders ask the congregation to sit for worship. I have experienced this behavior in some churches and I strongly believe that it's out of ignorance. You see, to them worship time is when the congregation should sit and enjoy the 'beautiful' voices of the choir and worship leaders. The fact that we are worshipping God does not resonate in their spirits. But then again, are they worshipping God? There is no anointing; the glory of God is not present in the atmosphere; the services are as dry as chips. It is really a sad state of affairs.

It's very disrespectful to sit during the time when we invite the Holy Spirit to be in our midst; to receive our corporate praise and worship; pay homage to Him and celebrate Him, our King of Kings and and Lord of Lords.

The Head of governments and other government dignitaries and so called celebrities are given more respect and more recognition than our heavenly Father Himself and the person of the Holy Spirit.

I have taught ushering and protocol for many years. As a result, I know that when the President or Prime Minister of a country makes an entrance into a function they are honored with a standing ovation, a drum roll and nobody is seated until he or she is seated first. So why do we treat the Almighty Holy One so shabbily when we are inviting Him in our midst. I know that He is everywhere, all the time, at the same time. He is Omnipresent. So some folks don't understand the concept of inviting Him in our presence and to experience His glory, His anointing, but it is real. It is my hope that before you finish reading this book you would have understood and experienced His presence.

It seems that some denominations do not fully understand what the Lord has done for us; the true extent of our salvation and how grateful we ought to be. We should read these scriptures again: ***John 3:16 and Isaiah 53:5-12***

He, who knew no sin ***(2Cor.5:21),*** took upon Himself our sins, our sicknesses, our infirmities, our fears, our troubles and *gave us the keys of the kingdom of heaven* ***(Matt. 16:19).*** In other words heaven is available for us to experience while we are right here on earth. We can enjoy 'kingdom living' right here on earth. We do not have to wait until we die and go to heaven. The kingdom of heaven is at hand, which means that we can now live in the spirit realm with our minds renewed and not in the soulish realm.

This way it becomes easy for us to **rejoice always,** seek His face, trust Him and acknowledge Him in all our ways. He bought us freedom and liberty and by His stripes we are healed, delivered, set free, restored and given authority over the enemy. Hallelujah!!!!!!!!

Some people attend church every Sunday and yet they have no sense of respect for God; no reverence, nothing. The whole purpose for 'assembling together' is lost in some churches where it's just a social club. You know I am speaking the truth. You go to church to meet your friends, eat and have fellowship/hangout. That's it. Well, the fact that you are reading this book means that you desire more, so you are forgiven. lol.

If we would understand and accept the fact that we, the people of God, are the church. The church is not the building. The building is where the church meets to be taught the word of God.

Heb. 10 : 25 *Do not forsake the assembling of yourselves together.*

When Jesus said that He will build His church and the gates of hell shall not prevail against it. **Matt 16:18** He was not talking about walls, doors and windows. We are the church and He, the Lord Himself is working on us if we would yield to His working. He is the Master Builder Who is ready and waiting to mold us and shape us into the kind of people He wants us to be. He will not force us, so He is waiting patiently for us to yield to Him.

So be vocal like one of the ten lepers in *Luke 17: 15-16 And one of them, when he saw that he was healed, turned back, and with **a loud voice glorified God,** and fell down on his face at His feet, giving Him thanks: and he was a Samaritan.*

Now if the Samaritan, who was not one of Jesus' people, could have recognized that after Jesus healed him, he needed to give Him thanks and glorify Him loudly, falling at His feet and worshiping Him, how much more should we **"the upright"** get out of our comfort zone and give Him praise and worship. **Yes, "praise *is comely* for the upright."**

I once had a friend (she is dead now) who was soft spoken most of the time. We attended about three different churches together and whenever the worship segment of the service came she would barely open her mouth or do anything else. I have no doubt whatsoever that she really loved the Lord. She claimed that she was always a reserved person and was having a hard time showing any emotion when she worshiped God. I, on the other hand, will always have a marvellous session of worship - rejoicing with dancing, clapping, singing, bowing before my Lord, just a joyful time in the presence of the King of Kings and Lord of Lords. I was giving God what was due to Him and at the same time I was making satan mad.

To me, it does not matter how soft spoken, dainty and sophisticated a person is, when it comes to praising God, the One True and Living One, the Almighty full of grace and mercy one, the Limitless One, He deserves our biggest shouts of praise.

One might ask the question: "Can we praise God in our minds?" Sure, we can and depending on the circumstances sometimes we have to praise silently. God can read our minds but the devil cannot, and we want the devil to hear us praise God even during the time that he is trying to put pressure on us. If you have a pain in your hand you can still lift it up and praise God that you have a hand: Saying, thank you Lord that I have hands because some people were born without hands and some have lost the use of theirs. Hallelujah, glory be to God!!!!

Back in Trinidad, we danced to almost every chorus in church, like it was nobody's business and it wasn't. It was between each individual and the Lord. We danced unto the Lord. Of course, we have the island rhythm. Even when I had just got saved in the early 1980s I attended one of the more progressive churches and in those days there was no dancing in church. But I could not let good music go to waste, so I danced. After a short time one of the deacons started hopping on one leg (that was his way of dancing) but some of the other deacons and elders ridiculed him for dancing. Eventually, there was a shift in the atmosphere and the whole church including the pastor was dancing unto the Lord.

Dance has been my weapon of war ever since. When I was under pressure and felt discouraged that's when I praised, worshipped and danced more than ever. Especially during the worship segment of the service at church.

I danced in the spirit and I danced in the natural. Sometimes while dancing in the natural, the anointing would come upon me and the Holy Spirit would take over and I would continue to dance in the spirit. Then, there were times when I decided that I was not going to dance and the Holy Spirit would take me out dancing and He would totally choreograph the dance. However, I always like to dance when I hear music. So during praise and worship I danced almost like David danced lol. Some people think that dancing **naturally** (in the soulish realm) in church is wrong and you have to wait on the Holy Spirit's unction to dance. No you don't. You dance because you want to rejoice and you want to celebrate Jesus. It is an act of your will. In so doing the anointing may or may not come upon you. Yes, I still dance, but not as much because in most cases the songs, the music, the atmosphere is not conducive to dancing and worshipping the way I did before.

I have never been to a club, but I have a fair idea from looking at the television and I have also seen 'disco-theques' on the television years ago. Some churches remind me of those scenarios with the dim lights, the flashing coloured lights, the rock music and just wild behaviour.

Let's not get too deep into the types of music because this book is about praise and worship, and not music per se. However, for me, it is very difficult to get into the presence of God in these circumstances. Difficult but not impossible. At those times I have had to dig deep into my spirit and with the help of the Holy Spirit I blank out my surroundings in order to engage in a one on one encounter with the Lord. Could you imagine what it would have been like if the whole congregation were to have that experience corporately?

The following scriptures are examples which answer the **'HOW'** question. They are very straightforward and to the point. Of course, the first one is where the Lord gave me the title for this book. It answers the **who, why and how** questions.

Psalm 33 : 1-3 *1* **Rejoice** *in the Lord o* **ye righteous**; *for* **praise is comely for the upright.**

2 **Praise the Lord with <u>harp</u>: <u>sing</u> unto Him with the <u>psaltery</u>** *and an* **instrument of <u>ten strings</u>.**

3 **Sing** *unto Him* **a new song; play <u>skilfully</u> with a <u>loud noise</u>**.

Ps.105:1-3 *1 O* **<u>give thanks</u>** *unto the Lord;* **<u>call upon his name</u>: <u>make known his deeds</u>** *among the people.*

2 **<u>Sing unto him</u>, <u>sing psalms</u>** *unto him:* **<u>talk ye of all his wondrous works.</u>**

3 ___Glory ye in his holy name___: *let the heart of them* ___rejoice___ *that seek the Lord.*

Phil 4:4 **Rejoice** *in the Lord* ___always:___ *and again I say,* **Rejoice.**

1Thess 5:16 Rejoice ___evermore___**. Pray without ceasing.** *In every thing* **give thanks:** *for this is the* **will of God in Christ Jesus** *concerning you.*

We are told to praise and thank Him with grateful hearts; call upon His name for He is the Great Provider and He has a name to match our every need; make a boast about Him and what He has done; **sing** to Him; give Him **glory**; **rejoice**; **play instruments loudly** and I don't know how to rejoice without **dancing**, especially with all the skillful music playing loudly.

Not only are we admonished in the bible to praise and worship God but we are taught **how** to do so. How do we behave, what do we do during the time of praise and worship, what should be the norm or '**comely' for the upright?**

Give Him glory and consider it an honour to be associated with Him and His name. The name that is above any other name, the name of Jesus. The **How** cannot be overemphasized. So I have added a few more passages of scripture that will hopefully get your attention.

Isaiah 12:4 - 6 *⁴And in that day <u>shall ye say</u>,* **Praise the Lord, call upon His name**, **declare His doings** *among the people,* **make mention that His name is exalted***.*

⁵Sing unto the Lord; *for He hath done excellent things: this is known in all the earth.*

⁶Cry out and shout, *thou inhabitant of Zion: for great is the Holy One of Israel in the midst of thee.*

In addition to what Psalm 105 says, **Isaiah 12** says to **<u>"cry out and shout"</u>**...

When I hear cry out and shout I immediately envisage love, joy, gladness, enthusiasm and triumph coming from deep within my spirit towards my Lord. It does not mean cry out and boohoo but instead it refers to gladness and excitement that should be experienced when we realize that the Holy One, the Righteous One who dwells within us and is among us and He is great. It reminds me of Moses and the children of Israel after their triumph and victory in crossing the red sea. *Exodus 15:1-21* It was indeed natural for them to give God praise and thanks. They composed a hymn of praise to God, using words that described the very situation from which they had escaped and how grateful they were to God for their deliverance. **Indeed, Praise is comely for the upright!**

Ps. 47:1 O <u>clap your hands</u>, all ye people; **<u>shout unto God</u>** *with the* **<u>voice of triumph</u>***.*

Ps. 95:1-2 1 O come, let us **sing unto the Lord:** let us **make a joyful noise** to the rock of our salvation.

2 Let us come before His presence with **thanksgiving,** and make a **joyful noise** unto Him **with psalms.**

Ps. 81:1-3   1 Sing aloud unto God our strength; **make a joyful noise** unto the God of Jacob.

2 Take **a psalm,** and bring hither **the timbrel,** the pleasant **harp with the psaltery. 3 Blow up the trumpet** in the new moon, in the time appointed, on our solemn feast day.

Here again, we are told to not only sing aloud and make a joyful noise but also to get some words from the Psalms and put some music to it. Bring out all your musical instruments, the timbrel, harp, psaltery, blow up the trumpet, play string instruments and in modern times we have organs, pianos, steel pans and many more.

2 Samuel 6:5 And David and all the house of Israel played before the Lord on **all manner of instruments** made of **fir wood,** even on **harps,** and on **psalteries,** and on **timbrels,** and on **cornets,** and on **cymbals.**

Ps. 98:4-6 4 **Make a joyful noise unto the Lord,** all the earth: make a loud noise, and rejoice, and sing praise.

5 Sing unto the Lord with the harp; with the harp, and the voice of a psalm.

6 *With trumpets and sound of cornet **make a joyful noise before the Lord, the King.***

***Ps. 100 Make a joyful noise** unto the Lord, all ye lands.*

*2 Serve the Lord with **gladness**: come before his presence with **singing**.*

3 Know ye that the Lord he is God: it is he that hath made us, and not we ourselves; we are his people, and the sheep of his pasture.

4 *Enter into his gates with **thanksgiving**, and into his courts with **praise: be thankful unto him, and bless his name.***

5 For the Lord is good; his mercy is everlasting; and his truth endureth to all generations.

***Ps. 66:1** Make a **joyful noise unto God**, all ye lands: Sing forth the honour of His name: make His praise glorious.*

With hands lifted up

Another articulation in praising and worshipping God is **With hands lifted up.**

1 Tim 2:8 *I will therefore that men **pray** everywhere, **lifting up holy hands**, without wrath and doubting.*

I know that this passage of scripture says '**pray** everywhere, **lifting up holy hands'** and we are dealing with praise and worship. Well, praying is talking to God. Praise and worship are different forms of praying. There is also thanksgiving, supplication, intercession and spiritual warfare.

Lifting up your hands is an act of surrender when we exercise our faith and trust in God with respect to a particular situation in our lives or when we are believing Him to have His way in every area of our lives. At this point, He can break us, melt us, mold us, fill us and use us for His honour and glory. So this scripture also supports lifting up our hands during praise and worship. In addition, it is a way of expressing thanks to God.

Ps.63:3 *Because thy lovingkindness is better than life, my lips shall praise thee. Thus will I bless thee while I live:* **I will lift up my hands in thy name.**

While I was giving a word of exhortation on praising God at a bible study, I was asked whether it was necessary to **lift your hands** and do all those things in order to praise God. Well, before I could answer someone else said "No", it is not necessary to lift hands, bow, speak, clap or any of those things during corporate 'praise and worship'. He intimated that he had been a worship leader at the church he attended for 14 years so he knew what he was talking about. Of course, he knew what he was speaking about concerning what was done in that church. However, he had no clue about praising and worshipping God.

He also said that at his church they sat during worship..

I chose the topic "Praise and Worship" because I did not believe that any christian would have an issue with praising God. Well, I had a rude awakening.

Ps. 134 : 2 Lift up your hands in the sanctuary and bless the Lord.

We could not get it any plainer than this. Lift up your hands **in the sanctuary** and bless/praise the Lord. This speaks about corporate praise and worship where the sanctuary may be filled with other members of the congregation. But we can have tunnel vision with our eyes, our hands, our minds and our whole beings focused on God.

CHAPTER 7
WHAT SHOULD WE SAY TO PRAISE GOD?

Develop your own praise song from your experiences. Coming from your own heart and soul. The words in the Psalms and other scriptures are expressions of how the psalmists, apostles, prophets and authors of the scriptures felt in their hearts about God. We know that the scriptures are God-breathe those that fit your situation by all means use them. Lets not forget that the word of God is the sword of the spirit.

Very early in my christian walk I learned to praise God. I desired to know everything about serving God so I attended every crusade and conference and I had a pastor, who taught us from the bible on every subject and every topic for life and godliness. I remember when he taught a series on "Praise". The scriptures were basically taken from the Book of Psalms.

This brings me to **WHAT** is being sung in some churches for praise and worship.

Some of the songs being sung today are contrary to the word of God. However, most 'church goers' either do not know the 'word' or feel that because it is being sung in church it's alright. What is more worrisome to me is that the pastors allow these things to happen without correction.

When we sing songs that do not line up with God's word we make the devil happy. After all, he is the one who tricks the songwriter into writing those lyrics. It is virtually impossible to compose a true worship/praise song without the anointing of the Holy Spirit. Hence the reason, we should be careful. Words are very powerful. You should mean what you say and say what you mean. If you do not mean it, then do not say it or even sing it. If I do not identify with a song that is sung in church, I do not sing it. So what do you do? Glad you asked. While everyone else is singing the unscriptural song I pray or sing in tongues. (That is the Holy Spirit's language).

I attended a church not very long ago where they sang 'worship' songs with words like: **"Lord, wreck me with your love'; 'spirits coming up from the ground'; 'Lord come close to me I am not moving, I am waiting right here, come to me Lord'.**

Firstly, the word 'wreck' as a verb, means to destroy; as a noun means destruction. So why would anyone ask God to destroy them and worst of all do it with His love. It just does not make sense. His desire is for us to have abundant life. A life of peace, joy, health, strength, love and prosperity among other things that are good for life and godliness.

John 10:10 *The **thief** cometh not, but for to steal, and to kill, and to **destroy: I am come** that they might **have life**, and that they might have it **more abundantly.***

John 3:16 For God so loved** the world that **He gave** His only begotten son that whosoever believeth in Him shall **not perish but have eternal life."

Of course, **God does not only Love us but He is LOVE.**

Then there was another song that referred to spirits that come 'up from the ground', really? The only spirit that I want on me is the Holy Spirit. The anointing comes from Him and flows down. ***Ps. 133:2*** *It is like the precious ointment **upon the head,** that ran **down upon the beard**, even **Aaron's beard**, that went **down to the skirts of his garments;***

Then, God's word tells us that we should ***draw nigh to Him and He will draw nigh to us***. ***James 4:8*** How could we be so presumptuous to tell Him that He should come to us instead because we are not moving; we are waiting for His move. Don't get me wrong, I know that they meant well and thought that they were being very 'spiritual'. The word of God is our sword. It is a part of our armour to fight against the enemy. So his, satan's strategy, is to cause God's people to say and do things that are contrary to the 'word' and he takes that opportunity as an open door and he infiltrates our praises and makes them of no effect.

Beware and be aware, 'try the spirits' ***1 John***

4:1 Beloved, believe not every spirit, but try the spirits whether they are of God:

There are christians who have been saved for many years and have real problems when they are asked to praise God. The only words of praise that they can utter is: Praise the Lord; hallelujah; thank you Jesus. Praise the Lord; hallelujah; thank you Jesus. That's it. They do not know any other words to acknowledge God and give Him praise. I usually direct folks like that and new believers to the book of Psalms. It's the best place to start when you want to learn the words to say to give Him praise.

Eph.5:19 Speaking to yourselves in **psalms** *and* **hymns** *and* **spiritual songs**, *singing and making melody in your heart to the Lord;*

In most instances, when asked to give God a clap offering most persons will simply clap slightly. I suggest some rigorous clapping with excitement while shouting some words of praise. What about 'give God a high note of praise' and people shout **"Whoaaaaaaaaaaaaaaa"** without any words of praise or thanksgiving. Then comes superbowl Sunday and you can hear much louder shouts and clapping with exuberance and excitement in nearly every household and club house etc. in the United States. Come on, Our God deserves way, way, more than that.

Praise Party

I remember back in the day, in Trinidad, at the church that I attended for over twenty years when the pastor announced that there was going to be a **praise party for the youths**. You should understand that the youths were the young people between 13 years old and 35 years old and then there were the 'young at heart'. Those who were older and felt young; like yours truly.

OMG it was awesome! All the pews were pushed along the walls and a big empty space was left like a dancehall. After prayer and words of exhortation from the pastor, the music began with praise choruses. We were all singing, dancing and praising God with loud voices and hands lifted up. Soon enough it became so intense that the anointing filled the atmosphere and some of those young people were on their knees with their hands in the air, others prostrated with their faces to the ground, some were obviously drunk in the spirit and just sat anywhere. It indeed, was a sight to behold. Then came the prophetic utterances and hearts crying out in surrender to the Lord. It was one of those **moments in time.**

Here are some suggestions as to **what** we can say when giving God **praise** and **thanks** and even unto **worship**.

I believe that we should always start with **praise and thanksgiving**

Ps.100:4 Enter into His gates with thanksgiving, and into His courts with praise: be thankful unto Him,

and bless His name.

It is very likely that some of us might be of the opinion that His gates and His courts are referring to the physical church gates and doors. So we are to enter the church property and go through the doors with thanksgiving and praise. Now do not misunderstand. It is a good thing to praise and thank God when entering the church anyhow but that scripture refers to spiritual gates and courts. Entering into His presence, at the time of devotion or prayer time or quiet time or intercessory time, anytime is praise time.

So here we go, **what**: Look into the scriptures both Old and New Testaments, especially the book of Psalms.

Hallelujah!

Glory be to God!

Praise the Lord!

Bless the Lord oh my soul and all that is within me bless His Holy Name!

Thank you Lord for your faithfulness, your loving kindness and your tender mercies!

Thank you for your mercies which are new every morning!

Thanks for your grace! Your grace is sufficient for me!

God, You are good and your mercies endureth forever!

Our Father Who Art in heaven, HALLOWED BE THY NAME – (speaks of His integrity)

Thank you for your love, your loving kindness is better than life

Thank you for the breath of life today

Thank You for the dawning of a brand new day.

This is the day that You have made, I will rejoice and be glad in it.

Thank you Father for sending Your only begotten Son, Jesus Christ, to die in my place **Jh.3:16**

Thank You, Jesus that You came, suffered, died and rose from the grave so that I might live.

Thank You, Jesus for shedding Your Blood for me.

There is power in the blood of Jesus; there is healing in the Blood of Jesus; there is deliverance in the blood of Jesus. Thank you Lord for your blood!

Thank you Jesus! You were wounded for my transgressions, bruised for my iniquities, the chastisement of my peace was upon you and by your stripes I am healed. **Isaiah 53:5**

Thank you Lord for making me whole. I am delivered. I have been set free.

Thank You, Holy Spirit for bringing honour and glory to His Name

I love You, Father, because You first loved me. **1Jh. 4:19** You sent your Son, Jesus, to die in my place.

Thank you Holy Spirit, You are my comforter, my teacher, my guardian, my guide, my strong tower.

Thank You, Holy Spirit, You prop me on every bending side, You are my Shield and Buckler; my help in ages past my hope for years to come.

Lord, You are great and greatly to be praised; Your greatness is unsearchable **Ps. 154:3**

Some trust in chariots and some in horses but I will remember the name of the Lord my God **Ps. 20:7**

Blessed be your name, Jesus. The name that is above every name. At your name every knee should bow, of things in heaven, and things in the earth, and things under the earth; And every tongue should confess that You are Lord, to the glory of God, the Father. **Phil. 2:10 - 11**

Lord, your name is a strong tower, the righteous runs into it and is safe. **Prov. 18:10**

Lord, I will praise You as long as I live, I will praise You while I have my being, my meditation of You shall be sweet, I will sing praises to You, Oh Lord.

Lord, You are Awesome; You are Mighty; You are Wonderful, You are the Prince of Peace; the Everlasting Father; the Roaring Lion in the Tribe of Judah; the Rose of Sharon; the Lily of the Valley; the Bright and Morning Star; You are the fairest of ten thousand to my soul, Hallelujah!

You are the Alpha and Omega; the beginning and the end; the first and the last **Rev.22:13**

You are the **Great I Am, the I Am, that I Am,** You are everything that I need.

You are from everlasting to everlasting

You are the Most High King. You are the King of kings and the Lord of lords!

Lord I will sing unto You as long as I live: I will sing praise to You, my God, while I have my being. My meditation of You shall be sweet: I will be glad in You, Oh Lord. **Ps.104:33**

They that wait upon the Lord shall renew their strength; they shall mount up with wings as eagles; they shall run, and not be weary; they shall walk, and not faint. **Isa. 40:31** Teach me Lord how to wait on you.

Thank you, Lord for making me a little lower than the angels. **Ps. 8:5**

I will love thee, O Lord, my strength. You are my rock, and my fortress, and my deliverer; my God, in whom I will trust; my buckler, and the horn of my salvation, and my strong tower. I will call upon you, Lord, you are worthy to be praised: so shall I be saved from mine enemies. *Ps. 18:1-3*

Thank you Jesus for salvation, redemption, peace, health and strength, healing and deliverance.

Thank you, Jesus, for making intercession for me at the right hand of the Father.

Thank you, Father that I am seated with Christ in heavenly places.

I am redeemed by the blood of the Lamb.

Thank you, Lord, that I am a victor and not a victim; I am above and not beneath; I am more than a conqueror in Christ Jesus;

Thank you Lord, I am an overcomer, I overcome by the blood of the Lamb and the word of my testimony. Hallelujah! **Rev. 12:11**

Lord, I thank You that greater are You in me than he who is in the world.

I adore you in spite of the circumstances, I adore You in the lion's den; I adore You in the fire; I praise You in the fire.

Father, You deserve my worship.

During my worship, I use the various names of God which signify His glory, nature, character, attributes, dominion and power.

Jehovah has seven compound names that reveal Him as meeting every need of man.

Jehovah Tsidkenu – The God of my righteousness, thank you that I am the righteousness of God in Christ Jesus **Jer.23:6**

Jehovah M'kaddesh – The God of my sanctification, thank you for setting me apart for such a time as this. **John 17:17-19**

Jehovah Shalom – The God of my peace, thank you for that deep settled peace. Thank you for giving me the peace that surpasses all understanding. **Judges 6:23**

Jehovah Shammah – The ever present God, Thank You always being with me. You promised to never leave me and You are not a man that You should lie. **Ezekiel 48:35**

Jehovah Rapha – You are the God that heals – The Mighty Healer – The Great Physician – thank You that no sickness or disease must dwell in my body because my body is Your temple. **Exodus 15:26**

Jehovah Jireh – My provider, thank You for supplying all my needs according to Your riches in glory by Christ Jesus. **Gen. 22:13-14; Phil.4:19** Thank You for being the source of my total supply.

Jehovah Nissi - My Banner, my protector, thank You for winning my battles; thank You for victory in Christ Jesus. **Exodus 17:8-15** The banner over me is love and you are love. I love you, Lord, because You first loved me.

Praise Him in your own words. Personalize the scriptures according to your experiences and your relationship with the Lord. Be genuine and sincere.

E.g. ***Psalm 91:3*** *Surely he shall **deliver thee** from the snare of the fowler, and from the noisome pestilence. He shall **cover thee** with his feathers, and under His wings **shalt thou trust**: His truth shall be **thy shield and buckler.***

I personalize it by saying **deliver me**, **cover me**, **shall I trust**, **my shield and buckler** and so on.

Prov. 27:21 *As the fining pot for silver, and the furnace for gold; so is a man to his praise.*

Refine your own praise by praising. As with anything else, the more you practice the better you become. Especially, when it is something you enjoy doing and it is coming from your heart. As we refine our praise, our praise will refine us. Continuous praise will refine the man, as the man refines his praise. Stop complaining and murmuring and begin to praise and thank God in every situation. Your life will change; sickness in your body will be healed; more people will be happy to be in your presence; you will become a more pleasant person within your own self .

CHAPTER 8

CONCLUSION - WHAT SHALL WE SAY THEN?
"PRAISE IS COMELY FOR THE UPRIGHT"

We have established that those that worship God must **worship Him in spirit and in truth.** This should be the right atmosphere for worship which is not necessarily the place where we worship but how we worship Him. The right attitude in our hearts/spirits; with clean hands and a pure heart; genuine and true.

As a lifestyle, it is building a relationship with God. Giving Him all the glory, all the honour and all the praise that is due to Him for what He has done for us. But more importantly **for Who He is** and because He is worthy of our praise and adoration. We see that our praise and adoration of Him does not affect Him because He is the same yesterday, today and forever. It affects us by changing our sadness to gladness. We are to put on the garment of praise for the spirit of heaviness. It is a good thing to **cultivate a lifestyle of thanksgiving and praise.**

Ps. 150 *Praise ye the Lord. Praise God in his sanctuary: praise him in the firmament of his power. Praise him for his mighty acts: praise him according to his excellent greatness. Praise him with the sound of the trumpet: praise him with the psaltery and harp. Praise him with the timbrel and dance: praise him with stringed instruments and organs. Praise him upon the loud cymbals: praise him upon the high sounding cymbals. Let every thing that hath breath praise the Lord. Praise ye the Lord.*

The last Psalm in the bible has encapsulated almost everything that has been mentioned before. It is we, the people of God, **who** are given the command/exhortation to **"praise the Lord"**. The angels in heaven are constantly worshipping Him because this is what they do. They understand who God is and what He is worth. As a matter of fact, when Lucifer was in heaven He was the master worshipper; he was the epitome of worship until he rebelled against God. Hence the reason he does not us to worship God.

As well as everything else that has breath. Things in heaven, things in the earth; those of us who have experienced His mighty acts; His excellent greatness should praise and exalt Him.

Where: In his sanctuary; in the firmament of His power

Why: For His mighty acts, according to His excellent greatness

How: with the sound of the trumpet; with the psaltery and harp; with the timbrel and dance; with stringed instruments and organs; upon the loud cymbals; upon the high sounding cymbals. Notice that this psalm starts with **who** and ends with **who.** *Let every thing that hath breath praise the Lord.* **Praise <u>ye</u> the Lord.**

Of course, other scriptures tell us to **stand, dance, sing, make some noise, clap, lift our hands, compose songs from the scriptures, make songs from our experiences like the children of Israel did with Moses, bow down before Him and just be in His presence.**

As a weapon of war

Eph. 6:12 *For* **we wrestle not against flesh and blood,** *but against principalities, against powers, against the rulers of the darkness of this world, against spiritual wickedness in high places.*

2 Cor. 10:3 & 4 *For though we walk in the flesh,* **we do not war after the flesh: (For the weapons of our warfare are not carnal,** *but mighty through God to the pulling down of strong holds;)* Of course, we cannot forget that the Lord took over the battle of Jerusalem under the leadership of King Jehoshaphat when they praised God. **2Chron 20:15, 21-22.** As well as when the Wall of Jericho fell. **Joshua 6:15- 16**

CHAPTER 9
A CALL TO WORSHIP

Psalm 95:6 O come, let us worship and bow down: let us kneel before the Lord our maker.

Individually and Corporately

The worship leaders should have the anointing to take the congregation from glory to glory in the Lord. The first criteria for joining the worship team should not be a good voice or the ability to play an instrument skillfully. The most important thing is that there has to be an anointing, a call on one's life to be a worshipper.

Mention was made earlier about the first time I taught at church on "Praise is comely for the upright" and there was a change in the way worship was conducted. Well, the worship leader immediately changed the lighting in the sanctuary. Dimmers were installed and soft light bulbs were put in place so that the atmosphere was changed into a more romantic setting during worship. He meant well, bless his heart, but did not understand that it was about the spirit rather than the sanctuary.

Responsibility of the Worship Leaders

We give **praise and thanks** to God because of what He has done, is doing and will do for us, and also for His promises to us in His word. However, **worship** involves itself with God Himself. Praise is moving up for God to do what He wants to do, while worship is fellowship with Him person to person. Worship is a step beyond praise. Praise is the cup and worship is the contents.

There are songs **about God** which are **neither praise nor worship songs.** Then there are praise and/or thanksgiving songs to God and there are songs of worship to God. Our Praise and Worship should be directed **to** God and not just **about** Him. e.g. I can say: "God is good" or I can say: "God, You are good". In the first example I am **talking about Him**. However, in the second example I am **talking to Him.**

The responsibility of 'worship leader' or the 'worship team' is to lead the congregation in worshipping God. It should not necessarily be about whether they have good singing voices, although that helps. I must say this: Whether you are leading worship, singing in the choir or singing solo, you are ministering. As such, should a new convert be allowed to minister and try to take the congregation into the presence of God? I say: No!

I remember as a church leader having a discussion with the other leaders concerning getting new converts/members involved in the activities of the church. Most of them felt that once the new believer was able to sing then joining the choir was one of the best areas for them to fit in. Needless to say I did not agree.

It does not matter how melodious they sound or how long they can hold a note. These positions are for mature believers who are filled with the Holy Ghost with the evidence of speaking in tongues and with power.

Satan was the worship leader in heaven. His name was Lucifer and he was the epitome of music. Of course, now he seeks to bring confusion and disrepute among the persons in the worship ministry. It is no wonder that the choirs and worship teams are almost always under attack. **A note to pastors:** Please have your intercessors to cover the ones in the music ministry as well.

The making of a worshipper

In **Exodus 13 & 14** we read about the children of Israel finally leaving Egypt. God went before them in a pillar of cloud by day and a pillar of fire by night. That in itself is a huge miracle. But as if that was not enough, Pharaoh and his army were pursuing them from behind, there were mountains on both sides and they were facing the sea.

As far as they were concerned they saw no way out. They were horrified and began murmuring against Moses and then they cried out to God.

Moses and the children of Israel sang a song of praise after crossing the Red Sea and seeing their enemies killed by one of the biggest miracles of their time. **They were changed from murmurers and became worshippers. Exodus 15:1-4, 11**

The woman with the alabaster box.

*Lk 7 : 37-38, 47-48 And, behold, a woman in the city, which was a sinner, when she knew that Jesus sat at meat in the Pharisee's house, brought an **alabaster box of ointment,** And stood at his feet behind him **weeping**, and began to **wash his feet with tears,** and **did wipe them with the hairs of her head,** and **kissed his feet**, and **anointed them with the ointment. V 47** Wherefore I say unto thee, **her sins,** which are many, **are forgiven;** for she loved much: but to whom little is forgiven, the same loveth little. And He said unto her, **Thy sins are forgiven.***

This woman offered tangible worship in the form of her tears, as well as her repentant heart and valuable perfume. Again, the more we realize the lost and hopeless condition we were in, the more we will appreciate what Christ has done for us and the more intense and real our worship ought to be.

Imagine she started out as a sinner **with many sins** and at the end of sincere worship her sins were forgiven. This tells me that an unsaved person who is moved by the Holy Spirit can also worship God with a sincere and repentant heart. Most likely that might be the time of their conversion.

In most instances, those of us who have been through the darkest times in our lives are the ones who tend to be true worshippers.

Here, I am using the Seven Levels Of Praise as our guide for this session of Praise and Worship.

The Seven Levels of Praise

The Seven Levels of Praise or Seven Manifestations of Praise. The terms for the different levels of praise to God are taken from the Hebrew Old Testament.

So let's get into corporate worship. It is Sunday morning and we are about to be led into worship by the worship leader/leaders.

As we move from one level to the next we sing and react according to the behaviour at that particular level. However, it should not be mechanical but instead should flow according to the anointing or leading of the Holy Spirit.

1. _Todah_ - Thanksgiving, lifting up of the hands, a sacrifice of praise.

At this first level you may want to sing a chorus or two of thanksgiving, while lifting up your hands and making a sacrifice of praise. It may really be a sacrifice for those persons who are not used to praising God or some who have come to church with the cares of the world on their minds. They will need a little time to focus on Our Lord. This is also as good a time as any to confess any transgressions that may hinder us from entering into **the Throne-room**.

Ps.141:2. *Let my prayer be set forth before thee as incense; and the lifting up of my hands as the evening sacrifice.*

2. _Yadah_ - Throw out your hands with all your strength and rejoice.

Ps. 134:2 *Lift up your hands in the sanctuary, and bless the LORD.*

Ps. 63:4 *Thus will I bless thee while I live: I will lift up my hands in thy name.*

Ps. 54:6 *I will freely sacrifice unto thee: I will praise thy name, O LORD; for it is good.*

Singing with a little more intensity, more purpose if you will. Lift your hands, dance and rejoice. Praise in accordance with the song that was sung.

3. _**Halal**_ **- Praise - To be clear, to shine; to celebrate; to show forth; to boast; to act clamorously foolish. Halal - Hallelujah - Halal to the Lord.**

Ps. 119:175 *Let my soul live, and it shall praise thee; (**our souls are ready**);*

Ps. 34:2 *My soul shall make her **boast in the Lord**: the humble shall hear thereof, and be glad.*

Ps. 115:18 *But we will bless the Lord from this time forth and for evermore. Praise the Lord..*

Exodus 15: 20 - 21 *And Miriam the prophetess, the sister of Aaron, took a timbrel in her hand; and all the women went out after her with timbrels and with dances. And Miriam answered tem, Sing ye to the Lord, for he hath triumphed gloriously; the horse and his rider hath he thrown into the sea.*

2 Samuel 6:14 *And David danced before the Lord with all his might; and David was girded with a linen ephod.*

I am picturing **Miriam** and the women in **Exodus 15: 20-21** and **David in 2 Sam. 6:14** and could imagine the clamorously foolish behaviour in both instances.

Sing appropriate songs to Him at this level. Praise, dance, rejoice, shout and clap.

4.   _Shabach_ - Praise - to address in a loud voice; tell Him what you want Him to do; to command; to triumph; to glory; to shout.

It's interesting that Shabach and Halal both mean to boast and are used interchangeably.

Ps. 117 reads: *"O praise **(halal)** the Lord, all ye nations: praise **(shabach)** Him all ye people."*

Ps. 63:3 *Because thy lovingkindness is better than life, my lips shall praise thee.*

Ps. 47:1 *O clap your hands, all ye people;* ***shout unto God with the voice of triumph.***

Ps. 35:1 - 2 *Plead my cause, O Lord, with them that strive with me: fight against them that fight against me. Take hold of shield and buckler, and stand up for mine help.*

By now, even while reading, you should be able to feel within your spirits, the change of the levels of praise. We are commanding what we want from God.

I must warn you here that your commands must be in keeping with the word of God. Words are powerful and we have the authority to say, to declare a thing and to prophesy over lives and our situations. Be careful what you ask for.

Sing appropriate songs to Him at this level. Praise, dance, rejoice, shout and clap.

5. _Zamar_ - To touch the strings, to play instruments, to let everything that hath breath praise the Lord.

Ps. 144:9 _I will **sing a new song unto thee, O God**: **upon a psaltery** and an **instrument of ten strings** will I sing praises unto thee._

Ps.104:33 _I will sing unto the LORD as long as I live: I will sing praise to my God while I have my being._

Ps 147:7 _Sing unto the Lord with thanksgiving;_ **sing praise upon the harp unto our God**:

1Cor.14:26 _How is it then, brethren? when ye come together, every one of you hath a psalm, hath a doctrine, hath a tongue, hath a revelation, hath an interpretation. Let all things be done unto edifying._

Ps. 150 Again, supports every level.

At this point, the musicians should be flowing under the anointing and allowing the Holy Spirit, Himself, to make music through them. Those instruments should be talking right now.

Sing appropriate songs to Him at this level. Praise, dance, rejoice, shout and clap. Let everything that hath breath praise the Lord!

6.   _Barak_ - The Lord responds in tangible ways, to adore, to bless; to be silent; to kneel in silence before God expecting to receive; hoping in God. He gives advice, encouragement and answers. He releases Himself to you.

Now we have moved from praise to **worship** where we are recognizing God not only for what He has done for us but also for who He is. We acknowledge His nature, attributes and ways by singing appropriate worship songs.

At this time, the **worship** has become more intense. Persons are kneeling, some are prostrating themselves before Him in humility. The music gets softer and totally spirit lead. Everyone is listening and expecting answers. Being sensitive to His leading. While He is dwelling in our praise healing and deliverance takes place. Answers are received; directions are given concerning ministry, business, relationships, and any other questions about different areas in our lives. He gives encouragement and advice. This is a good time to practice the art of listening to God. He is always talking but we do not hear because we do not listen.

Ps.22:3 *But thou art holy, O thou that inhabitest the praises of Israel.*

We must understand though, that for God to dwell in our praises, they must be genuine, coming from deep in our spirits, and overflowing through our mouths.

Ps. 95:6-7 (a) O come, let us worship and bow down: let us kneel before the Lord our maker. *For he is our God; and we are the people of his pasture, and the sheep of his hand.*

Psalm 72:12-15 *For He shall* **deliver the needy when he crieth**; *the* **poor also,** *and him that* **hath no helper**. *He shall spare the poor and needy, and shall save the souls of the needy. He shall* **redeem their soul from deceit and violence**: *and* **precious shall their blood be in His sight**. *And he shall live, and to him shall be* **given of the gold of Sheba**: **prayer** *also shall be made for him continually; and* **daily shall He be praised.**

7.   *Tehillah* – **To sing from your spirit, song of your spirit, residual song- the song of the spirit that lives in your spirit; it is always present in the believer.**

We have just entered into the Throne Room of God. There is very little direction from the pulpit at this time. The glory of God has filled the temple.

In the **Throne Room** miracles happen in His Name. The lame will walk; the blind will see; the deaf will hear; the anointing will fall upon some and they will begin to speak in the spirit language.

All christians should be filled with the Holy Spirit with the evidence of speaking in tongues which would also include singing in tongues, praising in tongues and prophesying.

Eph. 5:18-19 *And be not drunk with wine, wherein is excess; but be filled with the Spirit; Speaking to yourselves in psalms and hymns and spiritual songs, singing and making melody in your heart to the Lord;*

1 Corinthians 14:4 *He that speaketh in an unknown tongue edifieth himself;*

This is where prophetic worship is expressed. The delivering presence of God where we find rest and which is also a great weapon of war. The anointing is being poured out, so that the congregation will know that they are in the presence of God. As we shower Him with praises and worship Him, He comes and inhabits our praises. Praise or adoration is given to God that He, even with all His glory, comes and inhabits our praises.

Ps. 16:11 *Thou wilt shew me the path of life:* ***in thy presence is fullness of joy;***

Zeph 3:17 *The Lord thy God in the midst of thee is mighty; he will save, he will rejoice over thee with joy; he will rest in his love, he will joy over thee with singing.*

We have reached the highest dimension of praise and worship and there is a lot of excitement in His presence with singing, dancing, shouting, laughing, clapping, bowing, jumping, lifting of hands, shouts of hallelujah, glory, praise the Lord and it's all Holy Spirit led.

Some will sing a new song, others will be dancing in accordance with the leading of the spirit of God, while some will be drunk in the spirit and others will be making prophetic declarations and faith declarations regarding themselves and loved ones that will change their circumstances. Intercession and warfare have their places in the midst as well.

1 Cor. 14:26 *How is it then, brethren? when ye come together, every one of you hath a psalm, hath a doctrine, hath a tongue, hath a revelation, hath an interpretation. Let all things be done unto edifying.*

1 Peter 2:5 *Ye also, as lively stones, are built up a spiritual house, an holy priesthood, to offer up spiritual sacrifices, acceptable to God by Jesus Christ.*

Ps. 40:3 *And he hath put a new song in my mouth, even praise unto our God: many shall see it, and fear, and shall trust in the LORD.*

Acts 2:1 *And when the day of Pentecost was fully come, they were all with one accord in one place.*

2 Cor. 10:4 *For the weapons of our warfare are not carnal, but mighty through God to the pulling down of strong holds;*

Psalm 66:2 *Sing forth the honour of his name: make his praise glorious.*

God is calling the church today to a greater degree of worship; a greater degree of intimacy; a greater degree of glory. I believe that God expects a greater dimension in every area of our relationship with Him especially after this catastrophic year of 2020. Those of us who still have the breath of life in us remember that for us worship should be our **lifestyle.** Worshipping God is not only with our speech but also living in obedience to the Word of God.

1 Corinthians 14:40 *Let all things be done decently and in order.*

God's Throne-room

At least, Barak and Tehillah we should be in the Throne-room of God.

Where is God's Throne-room? God is a spirit and does not need a physical chair to sit. We know that a throne is a special seat for a monarch. So when the bible speaks of His throne its signifying His sovereign rule and not a literal chair.

a) **God's throne-room is a place of power and authority**

> ***2 Chronicles 18:18*** *Again he said, Therefore hear the word of the Lord; I saw the Lord sitting upon his throne, and all the host of heaven standing on his right hand and on his left.*

b. **God's throne-room is a place of majesty and honor.**

> **Hebrews 12:2** *Looking unto Jesus the author and finisher of our faith; who for the joy that was set before him endured the cross, despising the shame, and is **set down at the right hand of the throne of God.***

c. **God's throne-room is a place of sovereignty and holiness**

> ***Ps. 47:8*** *God reigneth over the heathen:* ***God sitteth upon the throne of his holiness****.*

d. **God's throne-room is a place of praise**

> ***Rev. 4:10-11*** *The **four and twenty elders fall down before Him that sat on the throne,** and **worship Him that liveth for ever and eve**r, and cast their crowns before the throne, saying, Thou art worthy, O Lord, to receive **glory and honour and power**: for thou hast created all things, and for thy pleasure they are and were created.*

Behold the beauty of the Lord and enquire in His temple. ***Ps. 27:4*** *One thing have I desired of the LORD, that will I seek after; that I may dwell in the house of the LORD all the days of my life, to behold the beauty of the LORD, and to enquire in his temple.*

Lord, what do you want me to do?

SURRENDER TO GOD; not my will but thine be done.

My soul says yes, yes Lord!

Yes to your will and yes to your way Lord!

I will say what you want me to say; I will hear what you want me to hear; I will go where you want me to go; I will do what you want me to do and I will be who you have called me to be.

It is very important to give the congregation time to praise between songs.

Yes, Praise is comely for the upright.